DAILY DU'AS

From When You Wake Up Until You Go To Bed

DU'A FOR WAKING UP

اَلْحَمْدُ لِلَّهِ الَّذِي عَافَانِي فِي جَسَدِي، وَرَدَّ عَلَيَّ رُوحِي، وَأَذِنَ لِي بِذِكْرِهِ

Alhamdu lillahil-lathee AAafanee fee jasadee waradda AAalayya roohee wa-athina lee bithikrih

> All praise is for Allah who restored to me my health and returned my soul and has allowed me to remember Him

DUA FOR ENTERING THE TOILET

(بِسْمِ اللَّهِ)
اللَّهُمَّ إِنِّي أَعُوذُ بِكَ مِنَ الْخُبْثِ وَالْخَبَائِثِ

(Bismil-lah)
allahumma innee aAAoothu bika minal-khubthi wal-khaba-ith

> (In the name of Allah)
> O Allah, I take refuge with you from all evil and evil-doers

DU'A FOR EXITING THE TOILET

غُفْرَانَكَ

Ghufranak

"I ask You (Allah) for forgiveness"

DU'A FOR BEFORE WUDU

بِسْمِ اللَّهِ

Bismil-lah

" In the name of Allah "

DU'A FOR AFTER WUDU

أَشْهَدُ أَنْ لَا إِلَهَ إِلاَّ اللهُ وَحْدَهُ لَا شَرِيكَ لَهُ وَأَشْهَدُ أَنَّ مُحَمَّداً عَبْدُهُ وَرَسُولُهُ

Ashhadu an la ilaha illal-lahu wahdahu la shareeka lah, wa-ashhadu anna Muhammadan AAabduhu warasooluh

> I bear witness that none has the right to be worshipped except Allah, alone without partner, and I bear witness that Muhammad is His slave and Messenger

DUA FOR GETTING DRESSED

الْحَمْدُ للهِ الَّذِي كَسَانِي هَذَا (الثَّوبَ) وَرَزَقَنِيهِ مِنْ غَيْرِ حَوْلٍ مِنِّي وَلَا قُوَّةٍ

Alhamdu lillaahil-lathee kasaanee haathaa (aththawba) wa razaqaneehi min ghayri hawlim-minnee wa laa quwwatin

> Praise is to Allah Who has clothed me with this (garment) and provided it for me, though I was powerless myself and incapable

DU'A FOR WEARING NEW CLOTHES

اللَّهُمَّ لَكَ الْحَمْدُ أَنْتَ كَسَوْتَنِيهِ، أَسْأَلُكَ مِنْ خَيْرِهِ وَخَيْرِ مَا صُنِعَ لَهُ، وَأَعُوذُ بِكَ مِنْ شَرِّهِ وَشَرِّ مَا صُنِعَ لَهُ

Allaahumma lakal-hamdu 'Anta kasawtaneehi, 'as'aluka min khayrihi wa khayri maa suni'a lahu, wa 'a'oothu bika min sharrihi wa sharri ma suni'a lahu

> O Allah, praise is to You. You have clothed me. I ask You for its goodness and the goodness of what it has been made for, and I seek Your protection from the evil of it and the evil of what it has been made for

DU'A FOR REMOVING CLOTHES

$$\text{بِسْمِ اللّٰهِ الَّذِي لَا إِلَهَ إِلَّا هُوَ}$$

Bismillahil ladhi la ilaha illa hu

> In the name of Allah, apart from whom there is no Lord

DU'A FOR EXITING THE HOUSE

بِسْمِ اللّٰهِ، تَوَكَّلْتُ عَلَى اللّٰهِ، وَلَا حَوْلَ وَلَا قُوَّةَ إِلَّا بِاللّٰهِ

Bismillaahi, tawakkaltu 'alallaahi, wa laa hawla wa laa quwwata illaa billaah

> In the Name of Allah, I have placed my trust in Allah; there is no might and no power except by Allah

DU'A FOR ENTERING THE HOUSE

بِسْمِ اللّٰهِ وَلَجْنَا، وَبِسْمِ اللّٰهِ خَرَجْنَا، وَعَلَى رَبِّنَا تَوَكَّلْنَا

Bismil-lahi walajna, wabismil-lahi kharajna, waAAala rabbina tawakkalna

> In the name of Allah we enter and in the name of Allah we leave, and upon our Lord we place our trust

DU'A UPON ENTERING MOSQUE

أَعوذُ بِاللّهِ العَظيمِ، وَبِوَجْهِهِ الكَرِيمِ وَسُلْطَانِه القَدِيمِ، مِنَ الشَّيْطَانِ الرَّجِيمِ، [بِسْمِ اللّٰهِ وَالصَّلَاةُ] [وَالسَّلامُ عَلَى رَسُولِ اللّٰهِ]، اَللَّهُمَّ افْتَحْ لِي أَبْوَابَ رَحْمَتِكَ

aAAoothu billahil-AAatheem wabiwajhihil-kareem wasultanihil-qadeem minash-shaytanir-rajeem, [bismil-lah, wassalatu] [wassalamu AAala rasoolil-lah], allahumma iftah lee abwaba rahmatik

> I take refuge with Allah, The Supreme and with His Noble Face, and His eternal authority from the accursed devil. In the name of Allah, and prayers and peace be upon the Messenger of Allah. O Allah, open the gates of Your mercy for me

DU'A UPON EXITING THE MOSQUE

بِسْمِ اللّهِ وَالصَّلاَةُ وَالسَّلاَمُ عَلَى رَسُولِ اللّهِ، اَللّهُمَّ إِنِّي أَسْأَلُكَ مِنْ فَضْلِكَ، اَللّهُمَّ اعْصِمْنِي مِنَ الشَّيْطَانِ الرَّجِيمِ

Bismil-lah wassalatu wassalamu AAala rasoolil-lah, allahumma innee as-aluka min fadlik, allahumma iAAsimnee minash-shaytanir-rajeem

> In the name of Allah, and prayers and peace be upon the Messenger of Allah. O Allah, I ask You from Your favour. O Allah, guard me from the accursed devil

DU'A FOR RIDING A VEHICLE

بِسْمِ اللهِ وَالْحَمْدُ لله، سُبْحانَ الّذي سَخَّرَ لَنا هذا وَما كُنّا لَهُ مُقْرِنين، وَإِنّا إِلى رَبِّنا لَمُنقَلِبون، الحَمْدُ لله، الحَمْدُ لله، الحَمْدُ لله، اللهُ أكْبَر، اللهُ أكْبَر، اللهُ أكْبَر، سُبحانَكَ اللّهُمَّ إِنّي ظَلَمْتُ نَفْسي فَاغْفِرْ لي، فَإِنَّهُ لا يَغْفِرُ الذُّنوبَ إِلاَّ أَنْت

bismillaah al-hamdu lillaahi, subhaan-alladhee sakhkhara lanaa haadhaa wa maa kunnaa lahu muqrineen, wa innaa ilaa rabbinaa la munqaliboon. al-hamdu lillaah, al-hamdu lillaah, al-hamdu lillaah, allaahu akbar, allaahu akbar, allaahu akbar, subhaanak-allaahumma innee halamtu nafsee faghfir lee, fa innahu laa yaghfir-udh-dhunooba illaa ant

DU'A FOR RIDING A VEHICLE

> With the Name of Allah. Praise is to Allah. Glory is to Him Who has provided this for us though we could never have had it by our efforts. Surely, unto our Lord we are returning. Praise is to Allah. Praise is to Allah. Praise is to Allah. Allah is the Most Great. Allah is the Most Great. Allah is the Most Great. Glory is to You. O Allah, I have wronged my own soul. Forgive me, for surely none forgives sins but You

DU'A BEFORE EATING & DRINKING

بِسْمِ اللَّهِ

Bismil-lah

> "In the name of Allah"

DU'A AFTER EATING & DRINKING

الْحَمْدُ لِلَّهِ الَّذِى اطْعَمَنَا وَسَقَانَا، وَجَعَلنَا مُسْلِمِينَ

Alhamdulilahil ladhi at'amana, wasaqana, waj'alna min-al Muslimeen

> Praise be to Allah Who has fed us and given us drink and made us Muslims

DUA BEFORE SLEEPING

بِاسْمِكَ رَبِّي وَضَعْتُ جَنْبِي، وَبِكَ أَرْفَعُهُ، فَإِنْ أَمْسَكْتَ نَفْسِي فَارْحَمْهَا، وَإِنْ أَرْسَلْتَهَا فَاحْفَظْهَا، بِمَا تَحْفَظُ بِهِ عِبَادَكَ الصَّالِحِينَ

Bismika rabbee wadaAAtu janbee wabika arfaAAuh, fa-in amsakta nafsee farhamha, wa-in arsaltaha fahfathha bima tahfathu bihi AAibadakas-saliheen

" In Your name my Lord, I lie down and in Your name I rise, so if You should take my soul then have mercy upon it, and if You should return my soul then protect it in the manner You do so with Your righteous servants "

DU'A FOR WAKING UP DURING THE NIGHT

لَا إِلَهَ إِلَّا اللهُ وَحْدَهُ لَا شَرِيكَ لَهُ ، لَهُ الْمُلْكُ وَلَهُ الْحَمْدُ ، وَهُوَ عَلَى كُلِّ شَيْءٍ قَدِيرٌ ، سُبْحَانَ اللهِ وَالْحَمْدُ لِلَّهِ ، وَلَا إِلَهَ إِلَّا اللهُ وَاللهُ أَكْبَرُ ، وَلَا حَوْلَ وَلَا قُوَّةَ إِلَّا بِاللهِ الْعَلِيِّ الْعَظِيمِ رَبِّ اغْفِرْ لِي

laa ilaaha ill-allaahu wahdahu laa shareeka lah, lahul-mulku wa lahul-hamd, wa huwa 'alaa kulli shay'in qadeer, subhaan-allaahi wal-hamdu lillaah, wa laa ilaaha ill-allaahu wallaahu akbar, wa laa hawla wa laa quwwata illaa billaahil-'aliyyil-'azeem rabbigh-fir leelaa ilaaha ill-allaahu wahdahu laa shareeka lah, lahul-mulku wa lahul-hamd, wa huwa 'alaa kulli shay'in qadeer, subhaan-allaahi wal-hamdu lillaah, wa laa ilaaha ill-allaahu wallaahu akbar, wa laa hawla wa laa quwwata illaa billaahil-'aliyyil-'azeem rabbigh-fir lee

DU'A FOR WAKING UP DURING THE NIGHT

"

None has the right to be worshipped except Allah, alone and with no partner, to Him belongs [all] sovereignty and praise, and He is able to do all things; How far from imperfections Allah is, and all praise is for Allah, and none has the right to be worshipped except Allah, Allah is the greatest, and there is no power nor might except with Allah, The Most High, The Supreme

"

FORGIVENESS

For when you have sinned

DU'A FOR FORGIVENESS

رَبِّ اِنِّىْ اَعُوْذُ بِكَ اَنْ اَسْـــَٔلَكَ مَا لَيْسَ لِيْ بِهٖ عِلْمٌ ۚ وَاِلَّا تَغْفِرْ لِيْ وَتَرْحَمْنِيْٓ اَكُنْ مِّنَ الْخٰسِرِيْنَ

Rabbi Inneee A-o'od'u Bika An As-alaka Maa Laysa Lee Bihee I'lm Wa Illaa Taghfirlee Wa Tarh'amneee Akum Minal Khaasireen

"O my Lord! I seek refuge with You from asking You that of which I have no knowledge. And unless You forgive me and have Mercy on me, I would indeed be one of the losers"

DU'A FOR FORGIVENESS

رَبِّ اغْفِرْ لِي رَبِّ اغْفِرْ لِي

Rabbighfir lee, Rabbighfir lee

"
My Lord, forgive me. My Lord, forgive me
"

DU'A FOR FORGIVENESS

اللَّهُمَّ اغْفِرْ لِي، وَارْحَمْنِي، وَاهْدِنِي، وَاجْبُرْنِي، وَعَافِنِي، وَارْزُقْنِي، وَارْفَعْنِي

Allaahum-maghfir lee, warhamnee, wahdinee, wajburnee, wa 'aafinee, warzuqnee, warfa'nee

"

O Allah forgive me, have mercy on me, guide me, support me, protect me, provide for me and elevate me

"

DU'A FOR FORGIVENESS

اللَّهُمَّ اغْفِرْ لِي ذَنْبِي كُلَّهُ، دِقَّهُ وَجِلَّهُ، وَأَوَّلَهُ وَآخِرَهُ وَعَلَانِيَتَهُ وَسِرَّهُ

Allaahum-maghfir lee thanbee kullahu, diqqahu wa jillahu, wa 'awwalahu wa 'aakhirahu wa 'alaaniyata hu wa sirrahu

"

O Allah, forgive me all my sins, great and small, the first and the last, those that are apparent and those that are hidden

"

DU'A FOR FORGIVENESS

اللَّهُمَّ إِنِّي ظَلَمْتُ نَفْسِي ظُلْماً كَثِيراً، وَلَا يَغْفِرُ الذُّنُوبَ إِلَّا أَنْتَ، فَاغْفِرْ لِي مَغْفِرَةً مِنْ عِنْدِكَ وَارْحَمْنِي إِنَّكَ أَنْتَ الْغَفُورُ الرَّحِيمُ

Allaahumma 'innee dhalamtu nafsee dhulman katheeran, wa laa yaghfiruth-thunooba 'illaa 'Anta, faghfir lee maghfiratan min 'indika warhamnee 'innaka 'Antal-Ghafoorur-Raheem

> O Allah, I have greatly wronged myself and no one forgives sins but You. So, grant me forgiveness and have mercy on me. Surely, you are Forgiving, Merciful

DU'A FOR FORGIVENESS

اللّهُمَّ إِنِّي أَسْـأَلُكَ بِرَحْمَتِكَ الَّتي وَسِعَت كُلَّ شيءٍ، أَنْ تَغْـفِرَ لِي

Allaahumma 'innee 'as'aluka birahmatikal-latee wasi'at kulla shay'in 'an taghfira lee

66

O Allah, I ask You by Your mercy, which encompasses all things, that You forgive me

99

DU'A FOR FORGIVENESS

رَبِّ اغْفِرْ لِي، وَتُبْ عَلَيَّ، إِنَّكَ أَنْتَ التَّوَّابُ الغَفُورُ

Rabbighfir lee wa tub 'alayya 'innaka 'Antat-Tawwaabul-Ghafoor

> My Lord, forgive me and accept my repentance, You are the Ever-Relenting, the All-Forgiving

HARDSHIP

For when you are facing difficulties

DU'A FOR HARDSHIP

لَّا إِلَٰهَ إِلَّا أَنتَ سُبْحَٰنَكَ إِنِّى كُنتُ مِنَ ٱلظَّٰلِمِينَ

la ilaha illa anta subhanaka inneekuntu mina aththalimeen

> There is no deity except You; exalted are You. Indeed, I have been of the wrongdoers

DU'A FOR HARDSHIP

اللهَّمَ إِنِّي أَعُوذُ بِكَ مِنْ جَهْدِ الْبَلَاءِ، وَدَرَكِ الشَّقَاءِ، وَسُوءِ الْقَضَاءِ، وَشَمَاتَةِ الْأَعْدَاءِ

Allaahumma 'innee 'a'oothu bika min jahdil-balaa'i, wa darakish-shaqaa'i, wa soo'il qadhaa'i, wa shamaatatil-'a'ada

> O Allah, I seek refuge in You from the anguish of tribulation, the lowest depths of misery, the bad of what is decreed and the malice of enemies

DU'A FOR HARDSHIP

يَا حَيُّ يَا قَيُّومُ بِرَحْمَتِكَ أَسْتَغِيثُ

Ya Hayyu Ya Qayyumu bi Rahmatika astaghith

" O the Ever living, the Sustainer, in your Mercy do I seek relief "

DU'A FOR HARDSHIP

ا إِلَهَ إِلَّا اللَّهُ الْعَظِيمُ الْحَلِيمُ ، لَا إِلَهَ إِلَّا اللَّهُ رَبُّ الْعَرْشِ الْعَظِيمِ ، لَا إِلَهَ إِلَّا اللَّهُ رَبُّ السَّمَوَاتِ وَرَبُّ الْأَرْضِ ، وَرَبُّ الْعَرْشِ الْكَرِيم

La ilaha illal-lahu Rabbul-l-'arsh il-'azim, La ilaha illallahu Rabbu-s-samawati wa Rabbu-l-ard, Rabbu-l-'arsh-il-Karim

> None has the right to be worshipped except Allah Forbearing. None has the right to be worshipped except Allah, Lord of the magnificent throne. None has the right to be worshipped except Allah, Lord of the Heavens, Lord of the Earth and Lord of the noble throne

DU'A FOR HARDSHIP

اللّهُمَّ لا سَهْلَ إلاّ ما جَعَلـتَهُ سَهـلاً، وَأَنْتَ تَجْعَلُ الْحَزَنَ إِذا شِئْتَ سَهْلاً

Allahumma la sahla Illa ma jaaltahu sahlan wa anta tajalul hazana idha shi'ta sahlan

O Allah there is no ease other than what you make easy. If You please You can ease sorrow

GRATITUDE

For when you are grateful for the blessings in your life

DU'A FOR GRATITUDE

رَبِّ أَوْزِعْنِي أَنْ أَشْكُرَ نِعْمَتَكَ الَّتِي أَنْعَمْتَ عَلَيَّ وَعَلَىٰ وَالِدَيَّ وَأَنْ أَعْمَلَ صَالِحًا تَرْضَاهُ وَأَصْلِحْ لِي فِي ذُرِّيَّتِي ۖ إِنِّي تُبْتُ إِلَيْكَ وَإِنِّي مِنَ الْمُسْلِمِينَ

Rabbi awzi'nee an ashkura ni'mataka allatee anAAamta AAalayya waAAalawalidayya waan aAAmala salihan tardahuwaaslih lee fee thurriyyatee innee tubtuilayka wa-innee mina almuslimeen

> My Lord, enable me to be grateful for Your favor which You have bestowed upon me and upon my parents and to work righteousness of which You will approve and make righteous for me my offspring. Indeed, I have repented to You, and indeed, I am of the Muslims

DU'A FOR GRATITUDE

رَبِّ أَوْزِعْنِي أَنْ أَشْكُرَ نِعْمَتَكَ الَّتِي أَنْعَمْتَ عَلَيَّ وَعَلَىٰ وَالِدَيَّ وَأَنْ أَعْمَلَ صَالِحًا تَرْضَاهُ وَأَدْخِلْنِي بِرَحْمَتِكَ فِي عِبَادِكَ الصَّالِحِينَ

Rabbi awziAAnee an ashkura niAAmataka allateeanAAamta AAalayya waAAala walidayya waan aAAmala salihantardahu waadkhilnee birahmatika fee AAibadikaassaliheen

> My Lord, enable me to be grateful for Your favor which You have bestowed upon me and upon my parents and to do righteousness of which You approve. And admit me by Your mercy into [the ranks of] Your righteous servants

DU'A FOR GRATITUDE

سُبْحَانَ رَبِّيَ الْعَظِيمِ

Subhaana Rabbiyal-'Adheem

"

Glory to my Lord the Exalted.

"

DU'A FOR GRATITUDE

الْحَمْدُ للهِ الَّذِي أَطْعَمَنَا وَسَقَانَا، وَكَفَانَا، وَآوَانَا، فَكَمْ مِمَّنْ لَا كَافِيَ لَهُ وَلَا مُؤْوِيَ

Alhamdu lillaahil-lathee 'at'amanaa wa saqaanaa, wa kafaanaa, wa 'aawaanaa, fakam mimman laa kaafiya lahu wa laa mu'wiya

> Praise is to Allah Who has provided us with food and with drink, sufficed us and gave us an abode for how many are there with no provision and no home

DU'A FOR GRATITUDE

الْحَمْدُ للهِ حَمْداً كَثِيراً طَيِّباً مُبارَكاً فيهِ، غَيْرَ مَكْفِيٍّ وَلا مُوَدَّعٍ وَلا مُسْتَغْنىً عَنْهُ رَبُّنا

Alhamdu lillahi hamdan katheeran tayyiban mubarakan feeh, ghayra makfiyyin wala muwaddaAAin, wala mustaghnan AAanhu rabbuna

> Allah be praised with an abundant beautiful blessed praise, a never-ending praise, a praise which we will never bid farewell to and an indispensable praise, He is our Lord

DU'A FOR GRATITUDE

سُبْحَانَ ذِي الْجَبَرُوتِ، وَالْمَلَكُوتِ، وَالْكِبْرِيَاءِ، وَالْعَظَمَةِ

Subhaana thil-jabarooti, walmalakooti, walkibriyaa'i, wal'adhamati

> Glory is to You, Master of power, of dominion, of majesty and greatness

Printed in Great Britain
by Amazon